IMAGES
of America

CHICAGO'S UPTOWN

Posted in front of this stately suburban mansion is a notice of its imminent demolition to make way for a luxurious, multistory apartment building. During the 1920s, this was a common occurrence in Uptown as the area's dramatic population growth facilitated the need for denser housing. (Courtesy of the Chicago History Museum.)

On the Cover: Uptown Station is pictured in 1922 not long after completion. From here, commuters could travel as far as Milwaukee. (CTA Collection, Illinois Railway Museum.)

IMAGES
of America

CHICAGO'S
UPTOWN

Jacob Lewis-Hall

ARCADIA
PUBLISHING

Copyright © 2024 by Jacob Lewis-Hall
ISBN 9781-4671-6141-1

Published by Arcadia Publishing
Charleston, South Carolina

Printed in the United States of America

Library of Congress Control Number: 2023950650

For all general information, please contact Arcadia Publishing:
Telephone 843-853-2070
Fax 843-853-0044
E-mail sales@arcadiapublishing.com

Visit us on the Internet at www.arcadiapublishing.com

This book is dedicated to Cornelius and George Rapp of Rapp
& Rapp, as well as Walter W. Ahschlager and the architectural
firm Huszagh & Hill. These imaginative architects helped steer
Uptown away from a reliance on Classical architecture and toward
the mélange of Revivalism and Art Deco I love so much.

Additional dedication goes to my ever-supportive husband and
grandmother, both of whom cheered me on throughout this journey.

CONTENTS

ACKNOWLEDGMENTS

This book would not be possible without the permission and cooperation of the archives at the Chicago History Museum and its Rights and Reproductions office. Unless otherwise noted, all images published here are given kind permission to be so by the Chicago History Museum. Special thanks also go to the Northside history team at the Sulzer Regional Library, Chicago Public Library, as well as the Research Center at the Art Institute of Chicago. None of this would have come to fruition if it had not been for the help, passion, and hard work of the people at these archives.

INTRODUCTION

Unlike most uptown districts in America's larger cities, Chicago's Uptown is not a continuation of its main downtown. Rather it grew about 8 miles north of the Loop, originally part of Lake View Township. Incorporated in 1857, the region that would become Uptown took its name from a small hotel called Lake View House. Opened in 1854, the hotel was considered a lakeside resort, attracting wealthy vacationers from all over the state, including US senator Steven Douglas and his new bride. In spite of the hotel's success, Lake View remained largely agrarian until the turn of the 20th century, developed mainly by Swedish and German immigrants who built modest farmhouses. In 1872, the Chicago, Milwaukee & St. Paul Railroad company built a commuter line between the Loop and Evanston, and development began in earnest. A second rail company would build directly parallel to this in 1900, terminating at the intersection of Wilson Avenue and Evanston Avenue (renamed Broadway in 1913). This became the epicenter of Uptown's meteoric growth. Additional streetcar lines only led to another surge in population, and by the end of the 1920s, what had only recently been farmland had become a densely urban core of entertainment, theaters, and shopping.

The onset of the Great Depression in the 1930s combined with wartime strain the following decade would ultimately stymie Uptown's good fortunes. Additional factors such as white flight and intentional divestment caused a rapid decline, and by the 1970s Uptown had garnered a seedy reputation. Urban Renewal projects displaced much-needed housing and services, leading to a rise in crime and homelessness in the area.

Much smaller than it once was, Uptown today is bound by Foster Avenue on the north, Irving Park Road and Montrose Avenue to the south, and Ravenswood Avenue on the west, while Lake Shore Drive and Lake Michigan hug the east. Its closest neighbors are Lake View, Andersonville, Edgewater, and Ravenswood. After the city released its official list of Community Areas in the late 1920s, Edgewater was considered part of Uptown. For a complex variety of reasons, residents of Edgewater pressured city hall to separate it from Uptown in the 1980s, which was granted.

This certainty did not help Uptown's reputation or economic fortunes, and it began to hemorrhage population for the first time. By the 2010s, the Graham Stewart Elementary School, once the most overcrowded of Chicago's public schools, was nearly empty and was subsequently closed by Mayor Rahm Emanuel amidst a slew of others.

Today, however, Uptown is experiencing something of a renaissance. In 2018, a multiyear project completely overhauling Wilson Station brought much-needed improvements to the aging infrastructure. Further north, stations at Lawrence and Argyle are receiving their own improvements as part of the CTA's Red/Purple Modernization project.

A Pan-Asian community known as Asia on Argyle thrives near Broadway and Argyle Avenue, while the Aragon Ballroom and Riviera Theater host a variety of rock and alternative music performers. Several construction projects are bringing much-needed housing to the neighborhood as renewed interest in the area brings new blood to Uptown.

One

RAPID URBANIZATION

Uptown's relationship to public transportation cannot be exaggerated. Before the rise of the automobile, trains allowed for development to spread farther from the city center than ever before. Giving rise to the "commuter," developers and boosters were eager to construct entire communities to meet the needs of this new type of consumer.

With the completion of the Chicago, Milwaukee & St. Paul Railroad (CM&SP) commuter line between the Loop and Evanston in 1872, several suburban stations were constructed in-between: Graceland-Buena Park, Sheridan Park, Argyle Park, and Edgewater, while everything east of Broadway was known as Cedar Lawn. Once Lake View was annexed into Chicago in the 1880s, access to transportation grew, and these disparate commuter suburbs would ultimately merge into Uptown.

In 1900, the Northwestern Elevated opened their own commuter railroad which ran parallel to the CM&SP's and terminated at Wilson Station at Wilson Avenue and Broadway. Streetcar lines along Lawrence Avenue, Clark Street, Broadway, and Montrose Avenue soon followed, allowing further connections between the soon-named Wilson Avenue District and downtown.

With this many choices in mass transportation, Uptown's population exploded, thanks in no small part to ambitious developers and boosters who saw the district's massive commercial potential. With lots selling for a fraction of those in the Loop, business owners jumped at the chance to construct shops, apartments, and theaters. In almost no time at all, the string of once sleepy commuter suburbs gave way to one of Chicago's busiest outlying commercial and entertainment districts.

In 1907, the Northwestern Elevated entered an agreement to utilize the Chicago, Milwaukee & St. Paul's existing, partially elevated tracks, replacing the latter's outmoded steam engine with modern electric service.

The following year, the Wilson Avenue terminal was converted into a through station, spurring another surge in development. By the middle of the next decade, the Northwestern's tracks had been completely elevated, freeing up space for street-level traffic while providing an even more direct line between Chicago and Evanston.

Looking north of Wilson Avenue down Evanston Avenue (Broadway) from the future site of the Northwestern Elevated tracks. In 1900, it scarcely resembles its Jazz Age self, with nothing but farmland and scattered forest as far as the eye can see. Within only a few years, this same view would become obscured by dense apartment buildings, small department stores, and luxurious hotels.

The Sheridan Park commuter station, formerly standing at Wilson and Clifton Avenues. The most elaborate of the Chicago, Milwaukee & St. Paul's commuter stations, Sheridan Park's ornate Romanesque architecture reflected the wealth of its residents. Famed Chicago architectural firm Holabird & Roche was commissioned to design the station, a further indication of the neighborhood's high status. By the 1920s, the station had been replaced by the Wilson Avenue Department Store.

The area around Sheridan Park Station in the very early 1900s. Still mostly rural, this same intersection would become unrecognizable in only a few decades, thanks to advances in public transportation. The station would be replaced with the Wilson Avenue Department Store in only 20 years or so, while the Clifton Theater was built next door. Already, streetcar tracks lace up and down Wilson Avenue while horse-drawn carriages trot alongside.

A northbound train pulls into the still unelevated Chicago, Milwaukee & St. Paul station. Alongside it is the now partially elevated Northwestern Elevated track. In the background, trees and vegetation are still clearly visible, indicating just how rural this area still was at the turn of the century. These boxy coal-powered train cars would soon be replaced by clean electric power courtesy of the Northwestern Elevated Railroad.

A southbound train travels along the recently elevated tracks above Argyle Street. This allowed trains to travel even faster between Evanston and the Loop, resulting in denser housing throughout Uptown. On either side of the tracks here are dense apartment blocks.

There was a time when horses powered streetcars. Pictured here are a team of two horses hitched up to a streetcar. While certainly slower than the later electric iterations, these horse-powered ones still allowed commuters to travel faster and farther than simply walking.

Much of Uptown's early development remained primarily suburban, with some wealthy families fleeing Chicago for what was still known as Lake View. This sumptuous, Italianate manor screams wealth with its wraparound front porch, pair of peaked roof gables, and elaborate flat-top tower surrounded by ornate bracketing. This opulent display of wealth was typical of homes from this late-1800s period.

SHERIDAN DRIVE ONE BLOCK SOUTH OF PATTINGTON.

Located near the Paddington Apartments, this stretch of Sheridan Road demonstrates the almost provincial character of early Buena Park. While already built up with apartment buildings and residential hotels, this section of Buena Park eschewed the standard Chicago street grid in favor of winding, European-style roads. This speaks to the neighborhood's origins as a lakeside respite for Chicago's wealthy families.

Many homes like these were treated as summer respites from the congestion and dirt of the city. Located mere blocks from Lake Michigan, these neighborhoods had an almost resort-like feel. This particular home, while relatively small compared to some, is surrounded by dense flora, a luxury after months spent in the congested urbanity of the city. Today, Buena Park and Sheridan Park are perhaps the best vestiges of this era, with quite a few of these luxurious suburban manors still surviving.

Children stare at the camera outside this imposing early Uptown home. Amidst copious amounts of shingling are splendid archways, an upper balcony with picturesque three-pane windows above it, and no less than three chimneys, which would have offered inhabitants warmth in nearly any part of the house. Before long, however, increased demand for dense housing following growth in public transportation would render this kind of sprawling estate obsolete.

Not all of Lake View's homes were quite as grand. Just as many were small but attractive cottages built by Swedish or German immigrants. While a tragic amount of these were demolished long ago, some survive today, such as this one pictured, thankfully with its rooftop cornice intact.

An unidentified woman and her three daughters sometime in the 1890s or early 1900s. Although her white shirtwaist and dark skirt were the standard woman's uniform of the day, her jaunty hat and lacy parasol indicate a woman of at least middle class. Her daughter's white dresses all appear well and starched, with bonnets laced to their curls with ribbons. Behind their mother, elaborate art glass and striped awnings make a stately first impression.

A large crowd gathered outside the Clarendon Municipal Bathing Beach Pavilion in 1916, during its first year in service. An incredibly handsome building, the Renaissance Revival pavilion offered a host of amenities that attracted over 425,000 paying beachgoers in its first year alone. At the pavilion, one could rent swimsuits, towels, and lockers, as well as access some of the finest shower facilities in the city at that time.

Bathing beaches became an increasingly popular venue for outdoor recreation in the last decade of the 19th century and early 20th. Shown here at Clarendon Beach, a woman warily stares down the camera as she pushes a large wicker pram along the dock. Behind her, children gaze off into the horizon over Lake Michigan while men in full suit and hat walk past. On the left-hand side in the distance is one of the city's water cribs.

Early bathing costumes for women were far less comfortable or practical than later iterations. Pictured in the 1890s, women play in the waters of Lake Michigan sporting bulky suits—essentially a short dress and leggings. Note that every one of them sports the same "cottage loaf" hairstyle, the signature coiffure of the decade.

A pair of young women play ball at Clarendon Avenue Beach in the 1910s. The beach's pavilion can be seen in the background, one of the city's finest outdoor facilities. A public beach, the nearby, private Wilson Beach offered far fewer amenities but was regardless the preference of Essanay Studio employees. Although not designated for them, they likely preferred the privacy it afforded.

Outdoor activities were incredibly popular during the first two decades of the 20th century. A 1919 boat race commences at the Wilson Avenue Bathing Beach. Some men are in business suits while others wear proper swimming outfits. Note the barricade between water, sand, and street, showing just how close to the lake development was at this time. In the background, a Jazz Age high-rise apartment towers above the festivities.

Elsie Luto (left) and Betty Blee (right) take in the sun and the surf at Wilson Avenue beach in 1929. For the first time in history, the suntan became a fashionable summertime accessory, communicating leisure and luxurious, far-off locations. A stark contrast to only 20 years prior, women's swimsuits by this time were far more practical and comfortable.

A group of teenagers fools around with one of the beach's rentable canoes as a lifeguard playfully chastises them. A far cry from the bulky suits and cottage loaf hair of their grandmothers, these young women enjoyed comfortable swimsuits and bobbed hair, much easier to manage for a day at the beach.

The 1920s also saw a big uptick in gadgets, as shown here. A group of children gather around as two lifeguards demonstrate how to use a respirator on a female volunteer. During this time, men's swimsuits were still one piece.

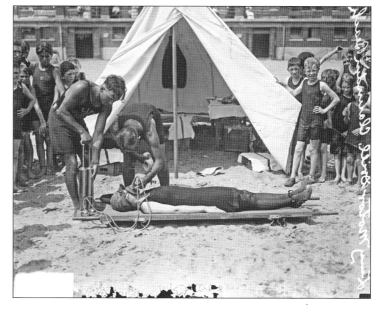

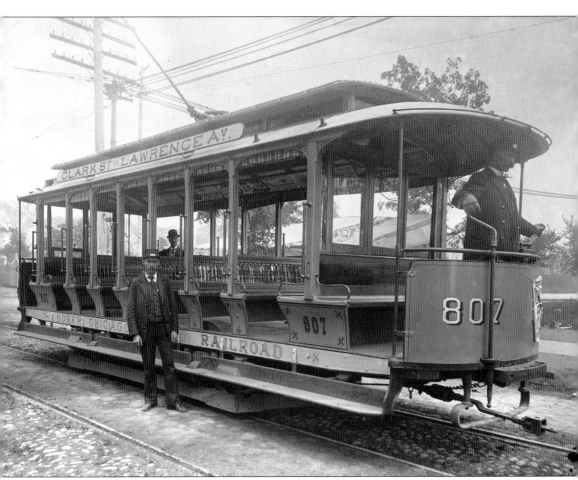

Advances in public transportation are what allowed Uptown to grow with such startling rapidity. Streetcars were just as integral to this process as the elevated tracks, with surface lines traveling north/south along Broadway and Clark Street, and still more going east/west down Lawrence Avenue and Wilson Avenue. Pictured here is a Lawrence-to-Clark streetcar operated by the North Chicago Railroad. Though still in its early phase, these surface lines allowed commuters to live farther away from work than ever before by ferrying them to and from the Loop with far greater expediency than a horse and buggy. One employee managed the steering equipment, while the other would have assisted riders. A lone commuter sits in the rear of the streetcar.

This photograph shows the future site of the Paddington Apartments. The rambling lake-side manor with its copious amount of private space and beach access demonstrates the character of early Uptown development. A lone boater rows just out of site. Today, this portion of the lake has been lost to Lake Shore Drive.

VIEW EAST OF PATTINGTON APARTMENTS.

Increased population meant an increase in demand for public services. Chief among these perhaps was the demand for clean drinking water, achieved by the installation of the pictured Wilson Avenue water crib. Located several miles out from the shore, the crib stored safe, clean drinking water for the residents of Uptown in tandem with an older crib east of Montrose Avenue.

One the country's only examples of a Prairie-style public school, Graeme Stewart Elementary was completed in 1907 a mere block or two away from Wilson Station. Built larger than necessary in anticipation of Uptown's growth, the school was at capacity in only a few years, with trailers required by the 1920s. The year 1940 saw the completion of a southern addition, but as Uptown became increasingly densely packed, the school became once again overstuffed. This would change as the neighborhood's population declined, culminating in the closure of Stewart Elementary in 2013. It has since been converted into expensive apartments.

Not all residents of the young neighborhood were reliant on public transit, however. Pictured here is another well-off family home with an automobile parked beneath the balconied porch. Still primarily seen as a pleasure vehicle for the rich, automobiles would soon take a toll on America's cities as they were torn apart to accommodate them.

No longer sparsely developed farmland, Uptown had grown into one of Chicago's densest neighborhoods by the 1920s. Here is depicted a typical cross street in Uptown, packed with apartment buildings and at least one residential hotel on the righthand side. The cohesion of architectural styles demonstrates the adage that buildings should "talk to each other," or be in some way harmonious with one another. While there is a small handful of automobiles parked curbside, it is nothing compared to the congestion we see today.

The snowy intersection of Broadway and Sheridan Road in the early 1900s. In only a few years, the Buena Memorial Presbyterian Church would replace the dense woods of this oddly shaped little peninsula. Situated between Buena Park and Sheridan Park, this particular slice of Uptown would remain in almost constant flux for nearly a century. (Courtesy of the Northside History Collection, Sulzer Regional Library, Chicago Public Library.)

Developer Sam Brown Jr. advertising the growth of Sheridan Park at Clark Street and Wilson Avenue. Pictured in April 1891, Lake View Township would have been only recently annexed into Chicago, which led to a surge in the construction of both homes and commercial real estate. (Courtesy of the Northside History Collection, Sulzer Regional Library, Chicago Public Library.)

Looking south down Magnolia Street from Wilson Avenue, and again down Beacon Street from Leland Avenue, the rural nature of pre-1900 Uptown becomes clear. Any surrounding land not utilized for farming was covered in dense wood. Even after the completion of the Sheridan Park commuter station in the 1870s, development was sparse and modest. (Courtesy of the Northside History Collection, Sulzer Regional Library, Chicago Public Library.)

As Uptown grew, its once suburban character was dwarfed by massive new developments. Here, a charming home is boxed in by a high-rise apartment building from the 1920s and another from the 1950s. The lack of windows on the side of the building to the left indicates builders anticipated a future apartment would be built, which, in this case, did not happen.

A fine example of Sheridan Park's early development, this mansion survives to this day at Wilson Avenue and Malden Street. An imposing Victorian edifice, its architect mashed together several popular styles of the day including Queen Anne, Classical Revival, and Flemish Revival, evident in its dramatic parapet. These types of homes were typically built on double lots, providing spacious yards and grounds. The urbanization of Uptown eventually saw many of these razzed in favor of denser apartment blocks.

This stately Victorian stick–style mansion was once located on Beacon Street at Sunnyside Avenue in Uptown's Sheridan Park. Another large suburban mansion, former Chicago mayor and Illinois governor Edward Fitzsimmons Dunne called it home for many years. A man of integrity, Dunne founded the National Unity Council in 1921 to combat the rise of the Ku Klux Klan in Chicago. His illustrious mansion was eventually torn down for a parking lot, but condominiums have since been erected in its place.

4331-35 Broadway & 4347-65 Sheridan Rd. Chicago. 14 10-16-51

Unrecognizable as the agrarian enclave of only a decade or two ago, the three-way intersection of Broadway, Montrose Avenue, and Sheridan Road is one of the neighborhood's busiest. A handsome three-story apartment building offers retail along its ground floor; this kind of mixed-use development was not only common before the rise of the automobile, but necessary in a dense, walkable neighborhood.

4331-35 Broadway & 4347-65 Sheridan Rd - Chgo. Ill 10-16-51

This commercial building at Sheridan Road and Broadway is typical of Uptown's early developments. Low rise and Classical Revival in architecture, developers were not yet willing to take risks in style, instead choosing more sedate but classic options. This one in particular is swathed in bright white limestone and terra-cotta, decorated along its roof with a faux balustrade and decorative urns.

Broadway

Montrose Ave

Plymouth's got

1331-35 Broadway + 4347-65 Sheridan Rd - Chgo. Ill - 10-16-51

Broadway north of Montrose Avenue in the 1940s is alive and thriving. Everything in sight was part of Uptown's early development, such as the mixed-use commercial apartment building on the right and the Arcadia Ballroom on the left. The Montrose Avenue streetcar tracks had not yet been cemented over, but would be by the end of the decade.

This building is another example of the Classical Revival character of pre-1925 Uptown. Also featuring a block of ground-floor retail below two stories of apartments, this commercial building must have been developed with middle- and upper-class consumers in mind. Creamy-white terra-cotta has been sculpted into a heavily bracketed frieze that peaks at each of the building's three parapets; below, more terra-cotta is shaped into decorative medallions.

A lone farmhouse sits at the southwest corner of Wilson Avenue and Broadway. Behind it, the Northwestern Railroad has already begun elevating its tracks north of Broadway. This humble house would be either moved or demolished not long after this photograph was taken, replaced with an entrance to the Wilson elevated station.

The small farmhouse is gone, as is any hint of the once-rural landscape. On the right stands the Stohr Arcade Building, commissioned by Peter C. Stohr, director of the Union Pacific Railroad. A young Frank Lloyd Wright was tasked with designing the retail/office building—no small feat given its narrow and awkward position beneath the elevated tracks. Wright cleverly tucked most of the building under these while allowing two stories to rise in front of them. Completed in 1907, the Stohr Arcade was demolished in 1922 to make way for Uptown's new Union station.

Looking north down Broadway from Wilson Avenue, the subtle detailing of Wright's work is more visible. A zigzag footprint creates a unique visual experience for those passing by, while the band of semicircle windows showcases Wright's Prairie-style flourish. H.O. Stone & Co., the National Tea Company, and a small market all occupy the space, while offices would have been located overhead.

Uptown from above in the late 1920s. Gone is any trace of the agrarian respite of only 20 years prior, giving way instead to dense urbanism. With Lake Shore Drive not yet extended this far north, Uptown's development closely hugged the shores of Lake Michigan. On the upper right, the Aquatania Apartments were built essentially on the beach, with occasional high tide creeping all the way up to the front entrance. In the distance stands the famous Edgewater Beach Hotel.

The change in Uptown's character from rural farmland to dense urban center is well summed up in this one photograph: in lieu of spacious country estates and suburban flora are a massive multistory apartment building, small neighborhood department store, and snarl of pedestrian, automobile, and streetcar traffic. The Uptown Federal Bank is visible on the far right, just one of a slew of financial institutions in the district.

By the 1920s, boosters such as architect Walter Ahlschlager were eagerly developing lots at bustling intersections. Located at the northeast corner of Wilson Avenue and Sheridan Road, Ahlschlager's imposing Sheridan Plaza Hotel was completed in 1921. Classical Revival in style, the hotel's elaborate, cream-colored terra-cotta ornamentation featured gargoyles, swag of fruits and flowers, and ornamental pinnacles along the roof. The first high rise in Uptown at that time, the Sheridan Plaza was built as a residential hotel, combining the concept of apartment living with the amenities of a hotel. Directly across Sheridan Road from the hotel was the Sheridan Recreation building, which housed a bowling alley, billiard hall, and at one time, the largest cafeteria in the world.

NORTH SHORE CONGREGATIONAL CHURCH, CHICAGO.
Patton & Miller, Architects.

THE INLAND ARCHITECT
AND NEWS RECORD
FEBRUARY, 1908

The first religious institution of note in Uptown, the North Shore Congregational Church was established in 1900. Made up of younger worshippers, the church grew with the neighborhood, and within only a few years needed a larger facility. After considering possible locations at Montrose Avenue and Lawrence Avenue, they finally selected a plumb spot at the intersection of Sheridan Road and Wilson Avenue. Architectural firm Patton & Miller designed the church's Gothic but modest edifice, pictured here in a 1908 copy of the *Inland Architect and News Record.* Today known as Uptown Baptist, the church's rooftop "Jesus Died for Your Sins" billboard has been something of a landmark for nearly a century. (Courtesy of the Ryerson and Burnham Art and Architecture Archives, Art Institute of Chicago.)

One of the first apartment buildings constructed in Uptown, the Fleur-de-lis opened to tenants in 1905 at Lawrence and Winthrop Avenues. Comprised of blonde brick and boasting a unique roofline, the Fleur-de-lis represents a pivotal shift in public perception of apartment living. Prior to this time, apartments had been looked down upon as less desirable than single-family homes. The answer was a new breed of stylish, attractive apartment buildings designed with middle and upper-class families in mind.

As time wore on, architects and developers started to construct more stately and elegant apartment buildings in Uptown. While nowhere near as opulent as the residential hotels of the 1920s, this first wave of rental properties was typically designed in classic styles meant to project the same air of wealth and prosperity as sprawling estates once had. The one pictured here, while only 3-stories, was completed in a Tudor Revival style, and featured elegant window bays framed by Doric columns. (Courtesy of the Ryerson and Burnham Art and Architecture Archives, Art Institute of Chicago.)

A typical Uptown apartment building from its heyday. Located at the corner of Sunnyside Avenue and Malden Street, this particular building represents the courtyard apartment, a style of apartment that was incredibly popular in Chicago during the early 1900s. Designed to allow renters plenty of light and fresh air, thousands of these apartments were constructed throughout the city during the early to mid-20th century in every imaginable architectural style. The courtyard pictured here combines elements of Classical with Palladian architecture, evident in its Solomonic columns and sculpted terra-cotta window lintels.

This dense but elegant Classical Revival apartment block at Wilson Avenue and Broadway was indicative of Uptown's early population surge. Built in the early 1900s, this building sports more terra-cotta sculpted into a bracketed frieze beneath a balustrade. Pictured here in the 1950s, this entire apartment building was demolished the following decade and replaced with a single-story commercial structure.

An advertisement for a stylish 12-story apartment building located on Junior Terrace in Buena Park. Its Beaux-Arts architecture would have complimented the surrounding single-family estates. Apartments ranged from four to ten rooms, which would have included the living room, kitchen, dining area, bathroom, and other rooms such as lounges or breakfast rooms, not just bedrooms. (Courtesy of the Ryerson and Burnham Art and Architecture Archives, Art Institute of Chicago.)

This image shows an unusual perspective of Broadway from behind Lower Wilson Station. Built in 1907, the charming Tudor architecture was executed by Arthur Gerber, the architect behind most of the Northwestern Railroad's elevated stations. Although intended to alleviate traffic congestion at Wilson Station, matters only worsened in the coming years.

A sizeable crowd gathers around the Stohrs Arcade Building in December 1922. Posted are signs announcing the construction of Uptown's new Union Station. Despite the implementation of Lower Wilson Station in the previous decade, rail traffic had only worsened, facilitating the need for a larger station. The new station would serve both the North Shore line as well as the Northwestern Elevated, today part of the Chicago Transit Authority Red Line. Once opened the following year, Uptown Station ushered in yet another era of growth for the neighborhood.

The recently completed Uptown Station gleams in white limestone as it peeks out from beneath the black and utilitarian elevated tracks. One of architect Arthur Gerber's largest transit projects, the station could meet all the needs of a small city's union station, offering luxuries such as a barber shop and lady's lounge in addition to carrying them as far from the Loop as Milwaukee. In front of the station stands a uniformed railroad employee, while on the left a small poster reads, "Arthur Gerber, Architect." (CTA Collection, Illinois Railway Museum.)

Uptown Station in 1924. Possibly one of Chicago's finest transit stations, Gerber spared no expense with this elegant fusion of Beaux Arts and Classical Revival details such as the rounded parapet inlaid with a large clock and highly decorated. "Uptown Station" was spelled out in seafoam-green raised terra-cotta, with Gerber's signature laurel-draped cartouches on either side of it. Despite the efficiency of the station, cars are parked all around it. (CTA Collection, Illinois Railway Museum.)

Uptown Station's lobby during Christmastime in the early 1920s. The decorative capitals of the columns, elaborate ceiling molding, and substantial pendant lights all lent an air of importance and dignity to the daily dredge of commuting. Large windows allowed for ample daylight to pour inside, showing off the terrazzo flooring. (Courtesy of the Illinois Railroad Museum's historic CTA archive.)

The barbershop inside Uptown Station in its earliest days, likely located in the basement. Several dour-looking barbers stand behind their chairs while one employee smiles for the camera. Even here, the low-slung ceiling is decorated with egg and dart molding and delicate electric lightbulbs, imparting a sense of dignity and elegance to even the most mundane of services. (Courtesy of the Illinois Railroad Museum's historic CTA archive.)

Two

A Times Square
for Chicago

It was not just advances in mass transportation that allowed Uptown to grow so quickly. Aggressive boosterism was another factor that led to the district's meteoric growth. Some of these boosters included architects like Marshall & Fox and Alfred Alschuler, as well as businessmen such as Loren Miller.

A former Marshall Field executive, Miller recognized the massive potential contained within the burgeoning district, leading him to purchase a plot of land in 1915 at Broadway and Leland Avenue just off Lawrence Avenue to build his own small-scale department store.

In fact, it was Miller himself who introduced the "Uptown" name, successfully campaigning to have the intersection of Broadway and Lawrence Avenue rechristened "Uptown Square" in 1930. While not a "town square" in the traditional sense, the name referenced the sheer confluence of shopping, entertainment, hotels, and office buildings present in the district.

Believing Uptown had the potential to become Chicago's own Times Square, Miller anchored it with his Loren Miller & Company department store, encouraging other business owners to follow suit. Before long, Broadway and Lawrence Avenue had usurped the Wilson Avenue district only two blocks south.

Coming of age at the dawn of cinema, Uptown was rife for theater development, beginning with the sedate Standard Vaudeville Theater on Wilson Avenue and ending with the bawdy Uptown Theater. By 1926, over two dozen movie houses operated in Uptown, in tandem with the sheer amount of hotels, restaurants, speakeasy bars, and other leisure activities, Uptown quickly grew to rival only the Loop as Chicago's entertainment destination.

Due to the sheer glut of housing options catering to such a wide range of incomes, rent in Uptown remained cheap for some time, inviting droves of young singles and recently married couples with more free time and disposable income than Americans had ever experienced.

Although the Great Depression quashed any notions Loren Miller had of Uptown becoming the city's Times Square, traces of his ambition linger to this day, making for one of Chicago's most distinct neighborhoods.

A bustling view of Broadway in the 1920s. Dominating the picture is the Arcadia Ballroom, one of Uptown's first large entertainment venues. Completed in 1910, dance organizer Paddy Harmon broke contemporary color lines by hiring all-Black jazz bands. This brought in massive crowds, quickly making the Arcadia one of the hottest spots on the North Side. With the 1926 opening of the lavish Aragon Ballroom, however, the Arcadia could not compete and served as both an ice rink and roller derby venue before burning down in the 1950s. A Target was finally built on the site in 2010.

An illustrative advertisement for Mann's Million Dollar Rainbo Gardens, once located on Clark Street just north of Lawrence Avenue and directly west of St. Boniface Cemetery. Opening its doors in the very early 1920s, the site of the Rainbo Gardens had long been one for recreation. Even before the dawn of streetcars, heavily trafficked intersections of the city's outer fringes were rife with roadside establishments. As these areas urbanized, some humble saloons and bars matured into thriving nightlife venues. Sadly, the Rainbo Room was torn down in the early 2000s after having become better known as a roller rink.

Another roadhouse that would see great success in the early years of the 20th century, the Green Mill Lounge first opened its doors in 1908 as a humble beer garden. In the years before World War I, outdoor drinking venues became incredibly popular, leading new management to heavily renovate, reopening as the Green Mill Gardens in 1911. Only four blocks from Essanay Studios, the Green Mill became a popular haunt for its actors. With the 1920 passing of the 18th Amendment banning the sale and consumption of alcohol, venues like the Green Mill suffered, many of them shuttering completely. Pictured here in the 1980s, its expansive outdoor beer garden had long been taken over by the Uptown Theater.

"Tied houses" were also popular during this time. Originating in England, tied houses gained popularity in Chicago after a misguided 1884 ordinance raised liquor licensing fees. In response, industrious brewers began sponsoring drinking houses in exchange for prominent advertising. The Milwaukee-based Schultz Brewery was perhaps the most successful in this venture, with several examples surviving today; this one was constructed in 1904 at Broadway and Winona Street. Featuring a prominent corner turret sporting a "witch's hat" roof, the German Renaissance Revival bar evoked the beer gardens of Germany.

The Argmore Theater, pictured here in the late 1930s or early 1940s. Completed in 1913, the Argmore represents the cinema house prior to the rise of movie palaces in the mid-1920s. Located at the corner of Argyle Street and Kenmore Avenue, the theater's name is a portmanteau of its intersection. As more illustrious theaters such as the Lakeside and Riviera opened the following decade, small affairs such as the Argmore simply could not compete. Fortunately, however, the building survives today as a retail space.

It would not be until 1925 that Uptown would receive its own true movie palace. Built atop the Green Mill's outdoor beer garden, famed theater architects Rapp & Rapp pulled out every stop for the positively palatial Uptown Theater. Boasting "an acre of seats in a magic city," the Uptown could seat 4,381 moviegoers in its massive auditorium, making it the largest theater in the world at the time. Inside, three separate lobbies allowed for nearly 9,000 patrons to enter at Broadway and exit at Lawrence or Magnolia Avenues simultaneously. (Courtesy of the Urban Remains image archive.)

Festooned in decadently sculpted terra-cotta provided by the American Terra Cotta Company, the Uptown Theater's exotic Spanish Baroque Revival architecture completely changed the aesthetic direction of Uptown's development. Sadly, the ornate rooftop "keyhole" parapet and decorative pinnacles were removed after the theater closed in the 1980s. (Courtesy of the Urban Remains image archive.)

One of the Uptown Theater's sumptuous hallways shortly after its 1925 opening. Heralded as the largest and most luxurious movie palace in the world, the Uptown featured ornately coffered ceilings, enormous chandeliers dripping in crystal decoration, heavy draperies over the windows and archways, and innumerable other details meant to dazzle moviegoers.

With Prohibition in full swing, dancing grew into one of America's favorite leisure activities. In response, developers commissioned architects to design elaborate dance venues, particularly in big cities. Completed in 1926, the dreamy Aragon Ballroom was designed by the architectural firm Huszagh & Hill, who would go on to design several key parts of Uptown Square.

Thanks to the Uptown Theater, Huszagh & Hill teamed up with theater architect John Ebberson to design the Aragon in a heady Spanish Moorish style. Located just steps from the Lawrence elevated train station at Lawrence and Kenmore Avenues, the Aragon Ballroom quickly became the hottest nightspot in Chicago.

Bricks arranged in a diamond pattern provide a backdrop for lavishly sculpted terra-cotta cartouches. Set beneath each are three faces, two of which depict beautiful women while the third shows a grotesque grin. A stylized swag of laurel, flowers, and fruits are painted bright but delicate shades of lavender and mint green. Even the small windows feature colorful glass squares.

The experience at the Aragon began before patrons even stepped foot inside. Pictured here is the ballroom's incredible front entrance with its bedizened coffered ceiling, fine crown molding, and wall mural depicting a ship at sea. Combined with the delicate shells carved into the terra-cotta ticket booths, the front entrance was meant to evoke the exoticism of the Spanish seaside.

The grand double staircase leads to the second-floor ballroom of the Aragon. Another extravagantly coffered ceiling shimmers above ornately carved banisters and imported Spanish tile. Two statues of dark-skinned men on either side of the staircase may raise eyebrows today, but in 1927, they were merely seen as another "exotic" ornamentation.

The main hallway of the Aragon leads from the entrance to the staircase. Rich details such as exposed wooden ceiling beams and a prolonged arcade of archways make even the mundane experience of walking from one place to another an exciting and beautiful part of the evening.

The actual ballroom was designed to resemble the outdoor courtyard of a Spanish villa. Beneath a blanket of artificial stars, dancers were transported across time and space to a fanciful world of escapism. A continuous rotunda allowed for 360-degree views of the dance floor, while a second-floor balcony offered lounge seating as a respite from the high-energy dancing.

The bustling intersection of Leland Avenue and Broadway. Dominating the streets are the Uptown Hotel, Loren Miller department store, Riviera Theater marquee on the left, and the Sheridan Trust & Savings Bank on the right. In the distance, the famous Green Mill Tavern and recently completed Uptown Theater are just visible. Automobiles weave around a streetcar, while shoppers meander on either side.

Completed in 1927 at Sheridan Road just west of Irving Park Road, the Sheridan Theater was another lavish movie palace built for the Uptown community. Located in the Buena Park section of Uptown, the Sheridan Theater was designed in a Greek Revival style by famed architect J.E.O. Pridmore. By the time this photograph was taken in the early 1950s, the theater had been sold and converted into a synagogue.

Even into the late 1930s and early 1940s, Uptown remained *the* entertainment destination in Chicago, eventually surpassing even the Loop. A beautiful example of late Art Deco/Art Moderne architecture, the Bowlium complex once again straddled the stretch between Sheridan Park and Buena Park, situated at Montrose Avenue and Broadway. The building's streamlined style reflects the impact that the Great Depression had on architecture. (Courtesy of the Ryerson and Burnham Art and Architecture Archives, Art Institute of Chicago.)

Looking east down Montrose Avenue from Broadway in the 1940s. Still a highly popular pastime, many bowling alleys were built as massive affairs with over a dozen lanes. Spanning nearly the entire block, Bowlium was eventually demolished and replaced by a Jewel Osco grocery store and parking lot. The Montrose Beach Hotel, visible in the foreground, was also torn down to make way for a high-rise senior home.

Like most of Uptown's prewar buildings, the Bowlium building was densely packed with shops and restaurants catering still to everyday residents as well as tourists. Marty's Shop for Men sold sportswear, Helling's served Chicago's famous roast beef, while William's Beauty Parlor, a dry cleaner, and a liquor store provided further revenue.

This is a glimpse inside Bowlium. In addition to theater-style seats for spectators, bowlers sat in comfortable leather booths. Before everything became computerized, patrons had to keep score manually with pencil and paper. Note the built-in ashtray in the center console, an indication of just how commonplace smoking once was. (Courtesy of the Ryerson and Burnham Art and Architecture Archives, Art Institute of Chicago.)

At the southern end of the complex was an A&P Supermarket, ironic given what would be built there decades later. From here the sleek lines of the Art Moderne structure are clearer than ever, offering a visual break from some of Uptown's louder architecture. (Courtesy of the Ryerson and Burnham Art and Architecture Archives, Art Institute of Chicago.)

Just south of the Bowlium complex in the 1940s, dense buildings were already being demolished to accommodate the automobile. Where a store or apartment building once stood is now occupied by a gas station. The Buena Oaks Hotel, located in the center of the image, was another early residential hotel in the neighborhood but has since been converted into a senior citizen center thanks to community advocates.

Even as early as the 1920s, urban developers were attempting to entice families from fleeing to the suburbs. Growing from the utilitarian apartment hotel, typically geared toward bachelors and migrant workers, these would expand in both size and prestige to become the sumptuous residential hotel. The first of its kind built in Uptown, the Sheridan Plaza Hotel was marketed toward families, offering all the luxurious amenities of a hotel including an in-house restaurant, ballroom, and daily maid service. The Sheridan Plaza remained one of the city's finest hotels for many decades before closing in the 1980s. Fortunately, it was soon after bought and turned into market-rate apartments.

While it may not be Times Square, looking north down Sheridan Road toward the Sheridan Plaza Hotel, it's easy to visualize Uptown as a thriving area for locals and visitors alike. Dominating the photograph is the Lakeland Hotel's building height, painted sign advertising furnished, kitchenette-equipped apartment hotel rooms, with special attention paid to tourists. On the left, a double-decker omnibus laden with passengers would have carried tourists to and from Uptown's biggest attractions.

At the southwest corner of Leland Avenue and Racine Avenue sits the sumptuous Leland Hotel. Built as another residential family hotel in 1927, architectural firm Dubin & Eisenberg channeled the nearby Uptown Theater in designing the Leland in an ornate Spanish Baroque style. Directly across the street is the Darlington Hotel, a Jazz Age addition to the 1909 Darling Apartments. Today, both the Leland and Darlington have been converted into stylish low-income housing, offering a bit of glamor to the families who need it most.

Not all apartment hotels were quite as grand, however. Just as many if not more were humble, such as the Hotel Stratford, pictured here likely in the 1960s. Another Spanish revival style, the Hotel Stratford eventually became a flop house before being converted into senior housing. Today, it survives as a straightforward apartment building.

Another example of a luxurious apartment hotel, the Wilton was another project by Huszagh & Hill, executed in a heady Venetian Gothic Revival style. Completed in 1926, the Wilton's rich design reflects the impact that the Uptown Theater had on the architectural character of Uptown. Although residential hotels by this time tended to be smaller, they typically more than made up for it with proximity to public transportation, shopping, and entertainment. Later renamed the Viceroy Hotel and again to the Lorali, the hotel wore many hats before finally being converted into apartments.

Perhaps the crown jewel of Uptown's residential hotels, the New Lawrence Hotel opened its doors to renters and hotel guests alike in 1928. Achingly modern in design, Huszagh & Hill broke with their revivalism trend in favor of high Art Deco. Swathed in limestone and black granite, the New Lawrence cut an imposing figure along Lawrence Avenue, with an elaborate cornice of figures carved to resemble sprites ringing the rooftop. Bronze window lintels were decorated with modern motifs such as zigzags and chevrons, further emphasizing the hotel's modernity. Eventually converted into a senior home, the former hotel has recently reopened as the Lawrence House apartments.

A cousin of the Argmore Theater, the Hotel Morland was another early fixture of Uptown's development. Likely designed by architect Thomas R. Bishop, the building's unique design harkens back to the neighborhood theater venues of yore. No longer a hotel, the former Morland is today part of the thriving Asia on Argyle neighborhood.

Before it was the Lakeland, the hotel on Sheridan Road just south of Wilson Avenue was known as the Lakeside. Not yet catering to tourists, the hotel still advertised its rooms and rates on the side of the building itself.

An advertisement for Weil-McClain plumbing fixtures. Pictured are several of Chicago's most illustrious apartment hotels, several of which were located in Uptown. Just as fixture and hardware companies tout their use in suburban homes today, apartment hotels were considered a lucrative enough market for which to do the same in the 1920s. (Courtesy of the Ryerson and Burnham Art and Architecture Archives, Art Institute of Chicago.)

A stylishly dressed young woman stands outside the Sheridan Plaza Hotel in 1929. With her fashionable fur coat, bobbed hair, and bare legs, she is the quintessential Uptown resident: modern, young, and with ample cash to spend on the latest trends and fads. Already dominating the streets, automobiles zoom south down Sheridan Road behind her.

Looking east down Wilson Avenue from Broadway in the mid-1920s, everything a resident or guest of Uptown could need is only a few feet away. If one were lodging in the Sheridan Plaza Hotel, for instance, one would be but steps away from a billiard hall/bowling alley, multiple restaurants, a lamp store, a shoe store, a butcher, a bakery, and even a piano retailer. This sort of dense confluence of retail catered to both residents and tourists.

Looking south down Broadway from the Uptown Theater in the very late 1920s, it is almost impossible to believe this same stretch of road only 20 years prior was a rural outpost several miles outside the Chicago city limits. On the left, the Sheridan Trust and Savings Bank had recently received a four-story addition, making it one of the tallest buildings in Uptown. Just to the right of this is the Loren Miller & Company department store, another anchor of the Uptown Square district.

With more and more Americans driving private automobiles, the city of Chicago voted in 1930 to extend Lake Shore Drive north from its then-terminus at Belmont Avenue. This tragically cut off much of Uptown from Lake Michigan, all but ending the district's reign as a prime beach destination. In conjunction with the 1929 onset of the Great Depression, Uptown's commercial growth began to slow considerably.

Three

THE LOOP'S
LITTLE BROTHER

By the 1920s, nearly two dozen commercial and entertainment districts thrived in Chicago's outlying neighborhoods. Sometimes referred to as "miniature Chicagos," these centers typically developed at major streetcar and elevated rail interchanges. The inevitable flow of pedestrian traffic lured business owners to intersections where frontage was much cheaper than in the Loop.

None of these could compete with Uptown Square at the intersection of Broadway and Lawrence Avenue. By the end of the 1920s, the Loop outpaced Uptown Square for its density of commercial and office buildings. Thanks in part to department store owner Loren Miller, by 1915 the triangular plot of land surrounded by Broadway, Lawrence Avenue, Leland Avenue, and Racine Avenue was completely developed with a hotel, department store, and bank.

These vital businesses, accessible to residents and tourists alike, helped usher in an era of commercial growth for the Uptown district. Within a decade, these businesses expanded into part of a bustling commercial corridor that spanned roughly along Broadway from Lawrence Avenue to Montrose Avenue at Sheridan Road. There were additional pockets in outlying districts, cropping up around individual elevated train stations. These catered more directly to urban commuters, stocking almost anything one may need as they dashed to and from the El.

Perhaps most notable was the Essanay Film Manufacturing Company, founded in 1907 by George Spoor and Gilbert Anderson. Before the rise of Hollywood in the 1920s, cities throughout the country vied for the opportunity to become the nation's filmmaking capital, with Chicago in the lead. By the 1910s, Essanay had constructed a new studio just west of the budding Uptown district at Argyle Street near Clark Street, a major north/west artery between the North Side and the Loop. The glamour brought on by Essanay brought additional patronage to Uptown, with local celebrities rooming in the Plymouth Hotel, dancing and drinking at the Green Mill Gardens.

In 1923, two large-scale office building projects were completed, solidifying Uptown as the most desirable location for businesses outside downtown. Thanks almost entirely to the rich confluence of public transit, companies such as the McJunkin Advertising Agency and Emerman Real Estate Company saw fit to construct massive office buildings at major intersection in Uptown. These would only grow by the end of the decade, ceasing only with the collapse of the economy in the 1929 stock market crash and ensuing Depression.

Most of Uptown's early businesses were small, family-run affairs such as the J.W. Schloesser & Co. Grocer and Market on Broadway near Wilson Avenue. Pictured here in the very early 1900s, a team of grocers and their horse-drawn carriages stand outside. The building's scale and Chicago Commercial style are typical of Uptown's early development. On top of the grocery is a Commonwealth Edison Company billboard advertising the newest craze: wiring one's home for electricity.

One of Uptown's smaller 1900s commercial developments, this humble single-story building on Broadway near Argyle Street featured Sullivanesque ornamentation in its parapet. Sculpted from terra-cotta, the ornate, organic decoration was reflective of architect Louis Sullivan's flowing, nature-inspired aesthetic. This style would fall out of favor with the rise of Art Deco in the 1920s. (Courtesy of the Ryerson and Burnham Art and Architecture Archives, Art Institute of Chicago.)

Located on Broadway between Leland and Wilson Avenues, this shop would have been erected in the early days of Uptown's growth. Faced in white terra-cotta, three sculpted medallions were set beneath a bracketed cornice. Pictured here in the 1990s or early 2000s, a wig shop had since taken up residence.

Servicing the Northwestern Elevated Railroad, the Wilson Shops were completed in 1901 atop the company's expansive Wilson Avenue rail yards. Despite additional yards eventually opening at Kimball and Howard, Wilson remained the primary stop for Northwestern's train cars to be serviced and maintained. The four-story commercial building would survive until the 1990s, after which it was demolished along with much of the rail yard.

Prior to the rise of Los Angeles as the world's film production capital, several American cities threw their own hat into the ring once the industry began to flee New York City. Founded in 1909, Essanay Studios was one of America's first and largest film studios. Begun by George Spoor and Gilbert Anderson, the studio was located on Argyle Street just east of Clark Street at the boundary between Uptown and Andersonville. Just four blocks from the Green Mill, many of the Essanay players frequented there before retiring home to the neighboring Uptown Hotel.

The actors of Essanay Studios pose for a group photograph in the 1910s. On the right-hand side near the front sits famed actor Charlie Chaplin, who called Chicago home briefly before settling In Los Angeles. Other prominent names of the young studio included Gloria Swanson and Wallace Beery. Several early Chaplin films were produced there before he succumbed to the mercurial Chicago weather and moved out west. Although Essanay sadly folded in 1917, its studio building survives to this day, now occupied by St. Augustine's College.

Originally built in 1912, the hotel at the corner of Leland Avenue and Broadway first opened as the Plymouth Hotel. Designed by architect George Kingsley, the Plymouth was one of Uptown's first high end hotels, and was called home by the likes of Gloria Swanson and Charlie Chaplin during their tenure at Essanay Studios. The hotel was later renamed to the Uptown before being purchased by the neighboring Loren Miller department store. After expanding into the defunct hotel, Miller sold his store to Goldblatt's, another Chicago-based chain.

This 1930s photograph depicts a chaotic scene on Broadway just south of Lawrence Avenue. A fire has broken out in the commercial building attached to the Sheridan Trust and Savings Bank, since renamed to the Uptown National Bank. Despite the impact of the Great Depression, Uptown Square is jam packed with streetcars and pedestrians. Even the alleyway on the righthand side of the image was once stuffed with shops and businesses.

Pictured here in the 1940s, the Cairo Supper Club was one of Chicago's scant examples of Egyptian Revival architecture. Executed in 1920 at the southern edge of Uptown in Buena Park, the fanciful commercial structure was the product of German architect Paul Gerhardt Sr. Originally constructed as an automobile showroom, it was soon converted into a supper club. (Courtesy of the Ryerson and Burnham Art and Architecture Archives, Art Institute of Chicago.)

The largest commercial structure erected in Uptown at the time, the McJunkin Building was commissioned by the McJunkin Advertising Agency. Completed in 1923 at the southwest corner of Broadway and Wilson Avenue, the prestigious firm of Marshall and Fox was behind the McJunkin's Beaux Arts/Classical Revival architecture, possibly in tandem with Arthur Gerber. Opening a year after the new Uptown Station, the McJunkin was designed to complement it and the nearby Wilson elevated station.

An older strip of commercial buildings at Wilson and Kenmore Avenues gave a strong impression of Uptown's early Classical Revival architecture. Pictured here in the 1970s, the once high-end stores have been replaced by pawn shops and check cashiers. Despite this, the white terra-cotta of the building in the foreground still gleams, its elaborate cornice thankfully intact. Looming in the distance, the Sheridan Plaza Hotel would remain open for only a few more years.

By the middle of the decade, the district east of Wilson Avenue and Broadway had truly come of age. Pictured here around 1925 at Sheridan Road near Wilson Avenue, it had already been overtaken by the burgeoning Uptown Square district just north down Broadway at Lawrence Avenue.

Located at the busy intersection of Lawrence Avenue and Sheridan Road, the Emerman Building came to represent Uptown's growing status as a viable alternative to the Loop for office buildings. Opening in 1922, the building's brilliant white, Classical Revival architecture was offset by the interior's "modern" amenities such as filtered drinking water and "air cooling." After four more floors were added in 1928, the Kemper Insurance Company entered a long-term lease with the Emerman, after which it became better known as the Mutual Insurance Building. Pictured here in the late 1920s, a Walgreens drugstore occupies the southwest corner commercial space. (Courtesy of the Ryerson and Burnham Art and Architecture Archives, Art Institute of Chicago.)

Following the 1925 completion of the Spanish Baroque Revival Uptown Theater, architects began to experiment with more flamboyant styles. The Uptown Broadway Building-shown here in the 1970s-was designed by Walter Ahlshlager in 1927 and is perhaps Uptown's best example of the massive shift in aesthetics after 1925. Described as a "Spanish Baroque hallucination," the Uptown Broadway Building's narrow footprint was made up for with excessive ornamentation and lively colors like yellow, pearl grey, and soft blue.

Decorated in sumptuously sculpted terra-cotta, Ahlslager imbued the Uptown Broadway Building with images of knight's helmets, mythological creatures, and symbols of wealth and plenty such as fruit. Ionic and twisted Solomonic columns make up the building's vertical window piers; the spandrels between them depict relief sculptures of faces and draped swag, while decorative urns top each of the buildings' columns. Providing a clear distinction between the heady revival styles of Uptown and the more sedate, classically inspired architecture of the Loop, architects created a distinct character for the younger district all its own.

A narrow commercial structure on Broadway just south of Lawrence Avenue and west of the nearby elevated train tracks is pictured in the 1970s. Having served many functions over the years, by this time it housed a bowling alley, advertising "LANES LANES LANES" above its front door. Its fanciful Mediterranean tiled roof had been removed by this time, possibly due to an earlier fire.

One of the first large-scale shops in the neighborhood, the Uptown Department Store was built atop the former Sheridan Park train station. Likely opened in the 1910s, it closed its doors barely a year later, unable to compete with Loren Miller's department store only two blocks north. It was soon after converted into the Wilson Club Men's Hotel, a men's only apartment hotel.

The Wilson Club is seen from the elevated Wilson station in the 1970s. Painted on the side of the building are the hotel's daily rates of 75¢ to $1 for a room. To the left of the hotel, the Clifton Theater had long since closed, with multiple retail spaces taking its place.

As Uptown's population surged in the 1910s and 1920s, it became necessary to retrofit already existing structures to meet the growing need for retail and services. Seen here at the northwest corner of Sheridan Road and Lawrence Avenue in the 1960s, one popular method of doing so was adding a "dickie front" to apartment buildings located at crucial intersections. This method of construction allowed developers to add commercial space without sacrificing housing. This example proves interesting, with the three-story apartment building being of a typical late-19th-century style and the dickie front designed to complement the Art Deco New Lawrence Hotel in the background.

The 1950s truly was Uptown's last gasp of commercial success before the economic downtown of the 20th century's latter half. Along Broadway between Wilson Avenue and Leland Avenue were multiple shops and offices leased out of some of Uptown's oldest commercial buildings. Below Dr. Weisbach's second-floor dentist's office was the Cotton Store clothing boutique, with a lingerie store to the left of that. Further down was a meat market, shoe store, bargain department store, and a menswear shop. Streetcar tracks were still visible along Broadway, while more and more cars packed the curb.

Looking east down Wilson Avenue from Racine Avenue in the 1950s. By this time, Uptown's good fortunes had begun to fade, leaving its once-thriving commercial districts looking worn and tattered. On the right, the De Lux Theater has resorted to showing Adult Films in addition to family fare in order to stay open. On the left-hand side, the upper floors of the former Clifton Theater have been converted into bachelor apartments, still an incredibly popular form of housing for men following World War II.

Amidst the throes of the Great Depression, the American government granted funds for the construction of much-needed public and municipal buildings across the country. The Loop received its own Art Moderne post office, but so did Uptown. Completed in 1939 by architect Howard Cheney, Uptown's United States Post Office was erected at the northwest corner of Broadway and Gunnison Street, just one block north of the Uptown Theater.

A stark contrast to the flamboyance of its terra-cotta-clad neighbors, the 1939 post office shows just how dramatically architecture responded to the 1929 stock market crash. Eschewing bawdy ornamentation in favor of sleek, aerodynamic lines, the new building was the first major construction project Uptown saw since the onset of the Depression. The building's front entrance featured a bank of three vertical window piers surrounded by plain brick. The only decoration present was a pair of sculpted eagles on either side of the stairway.

The Sheridan Trust & Savings Bank shortly after its 1924 completion. After outgrowing its former flagship across the street, the bank commissioned the prestigious firm of Marshall & Fox to design their new bank building at the southeast corner of Lawrence Avenue and Broadway. Although still Classical Revival in style, the influence of Art Deco is clear in the bank's geometric interpretation of Ionic columns and relief-decorated spandrels. Only four years later, the bank would receive a four-story addition. Like many banking institutions during the 1930s, Sheridan Trust & Savings succumbed to the Great Depression in 1931, after which it was taken over by the Uptown National Bank. (Courtesy of the Northwest Architectural Archive, Elmer L. Andersen Library, University of Minnesota.)

A view of Lawrence Avenue looking west from Broadway, On the left is the main floor of the Uptown National Bank, while on the right stands the Clancy Building, one of the oldest multistory commercial buildings in Uptown. Just ahead of it stands the Green Mill Lounge. Pictured here in the 1950s, Uptown would soon enter a period of prolonged decline from which it would not recover for many decades.

Four

HILLBILLY HEAVEN AND URBAN RENEWAL

While the exact cause of the Great Depression is debatable, the effects of the 1929 stock market crash were undeniable. Economies that relied on industry were the hardest hit, with Chicago being no exception.

Movie theaters, however, saw a surge in business as silent films gave way to "talkies," attracting larger audiences than ever before. Ballrooms such as the Aragon became more popular, as guests could purchase a ticket and enjoy an entire evening of entertainment. These attractions kept people coming to Uptown to spend what little cash they could spare. Additionally, the 1933 repeal of Prohibition allowed for the sale and consumption of alcohol, resulting in the Green Mill "reopening" as a cocktail lounge.

During the war years, soldiers stationed at Fort Sheridan and the Great Lakes Naval Training Station brought renewed interest to the entertainment district. The increased need for housing led many landlords to divide up large apartments and single-family houses into small kitchenette units. This led to yet another surge in population. This trend continued into the 1960s and 1970s, as tens of thousands of Native American and white Appalachian migrants poured into Uptown. By this time, Uptown's viability as Chicago's entertainment and retail destination had ended. The neighborhood entered a period of steep decline marked by flop houses, pawn shops, and poverty.

Then a well-known port of entry for immigrants, Uptown began to dawn a new identity as refugees from Vietnam, Korea, and Cambodia settled into the blocks surrounding the Argyle elevated station in the 1980s and 1990s. Typically referred to as "Asia on Argyle" or "Little Chinatown," the neighborhood would soon grow into one of Chicago's most distinct neighborhoods.

By the middle of the 20th century, newly constructed highways allowed white families to flee to the suburbs, leaving nothing but abject poverty in their wake. City neighborhoods began to fall into blight once these families took their tax dollars with them, creating slums even in some of Chicago's finest neighborhoods.

The government's response to this urban renewal consisted of nothing more than demolishing much needed housing in favor of parking lots, strip malls, and gas stations. This left an empty, hollowed out feeling in these areas, which only encouraged more well-to-do people to move out. While no part of Chicago was untouched, Uptown's decline occurred even faster than its inception.

With the worst of the Great Depression over and America not yet involved in World War II, Chicago saw dozens of new housing projects. The eight-story, 5040-5060 Marine Drive was designed by architectural firm Oman & Lilienthal and is a stunning example of Art Moderne architecture used residentially. Comprised of 203 units distributed amongst six staggered blocks maximizing views of Lake Michigan, the corner windows and multicolored stripes would have been seen as incredibly modern. (Courtesy of the Ryerson and Burnham Art and Architecture Archives, Art Institute of Chicago.)

4880 Marine Drive

4880 Marine Drive Building Corporation — Owners

Frank A. McNally and Associates — Architects

Madison Realty Company — Renting Agents

120 APARTMENTS

The property at 4880 Marine Drive, a postwar, mid-century development in Uptown, is shown here in a drawn advertisement. Around this period, the majority of construction projects hugged Lake Shore Drive, offering prime lake views for residents. Architectural firm Frank A. McNally and Associates delivered Uptown its first taste of Modernism, the straightforward and simple design sharply contrasting with the neighborhood's more historic structures. (Courtesy of the Ryerson and Burnham Art and Architecture Archives, Art Institute of Chicago.)

This 1960s stretch of Broadway between Wilson and Montrose Avenues formerly contained the Arcadia Ballroom but is now home to a gas station and car wash. The McJunkin Building is visible on the right, while the Wilson shops still survive on the left.

On Sheridan Road near the old Lakeside Hotel, an apartment building on the far righthand side was razed for a Shell gas station. Further up, dicky front shops have been converted to liquor stores and cheap bars, reflective of the rapid decline in Uptown's character.

At Sheridan Road and Wilson Avenue, the once-charming Sheridan Recreation complex was replaced with a drive-thru fast-food restaurant. This was a common sight in 1970s America, with Uptown being no exception.

Further north on Argyle, a beautiful Art Deco commercial structure has been taken over by a pharmacy. In addition to bars and liquor stores, social services such as low-cost medicine dispensaries began to crop up all over Uptown. Fortunately here, the buildings' ornate terra-cotta has been spared.

Hull House was founded in 1889 by social reformer Jane Addams to provide much-needed social services to recently arrived European Immigrants. By the 1920s, Hull House operated over 500 locations throughout the city. Pictured here in the 1970s, the Uptown branch of Hull House was opened on Beacon Street atop two former mansions. A group of children play outside, while a sign on the window advertises an open game room for them.

As early as the 1970s, immigrants from South Asia began to transform the area of Uptown around Broadway and Argyle Street. Seen here, the commercial space of a Classical Revival apartment building now hosts several Vietnamese businesses. This influx of new residents helped much of Argyle Street's architecture to avoid demolition.

Looking west down Wilson Avenue from beneath the elevated train tracks in the 1970s, it is easy to see how much Uptown has changed since its golden era 50 years prior. Now catering to a more transient population, nearly all the shops and hotels have decreased in quality.

Many buildings in Uptown were demolished to make way for needed public services. One such example, shown here in the 1970s, stood at Wilson and Racine Avenues. A commercial building and an apartment flat were torn down in favor of a neighborhood fire station.

Dense apartment blocks at Wilson Avenue, Beacon Street, and Malden Street are seen here in the 1970s. Their stately and elegant architecture spoke to the prestige of the neighborhood during the late 19th and early 20th centuries. Although still intact, their scrubby yards and utilitarian, chain-link fences communicate the early signs of urban decay.

Large apartment homes like these on Wilson Avenue at Beacon and Dover Streets were just the kind to be chopped up into substandard micro apartments in the post–World War II years. Where once spacious units housed Uptown's wealthy, dangerous flats wallpapered in newspaper and lit with naked lightbulbs took their place. This trend continued well into the 1980s until local activists demanded housing reform. (Both, courtesy of the Ryerson and Burnham Art and Architecture Archives, Art Institute of Chicago.)

To address the lack of advanced education on the North Side, city officials selected land adjacent to the Wilson elevated station to be razed in favor of a new community college. Bordered by Wilson Avenue to the north, Racine Avenue to the west, and Sunnyside Avenue to the south, the future site of Harry S. Truman City College was densely packed with apartments, residential hotels, corner shops, and social services communities. By the 1970s, this was torn down, with the Harry S. Truman City College having taken its place.

Completed in 1956 under the name Mayfair College, the new two-year school provided over 40,000 new jobs to the commercially ailing Uptown neighborhood. Rechristened Harry S. Truman College in 1976, the school offered courses in the sciences, child development, automotive and other mechanical fields, math, foreign languages and various vocational programs. By the 1960s, over 4,000 students were enrolled at the college.

Looking down Broadway from Leland Avenue in the 1990s, the downturn of Uptown is apparent. The bowling alley attached to the former Sheridan Trust & Savings Bank had long been demolished, while several retail spaces in the Uptown Broadway Building sit vacant. In the distance, the Uptown Theater's multistory marquee is empty, with the theater having closed the previous decade.

By the 1960s, many of Uptown's well-established businesses and companies had fled to the suburbs, leaving their old buildings empty. Even the once-illustrious Mutual Insurance Building was abandoned by Kemper Insurance, leaving it briefly vacant. Thankfully, Kemper soon after donated the building to a local nonprofit, which it remains in possession of to this day.

After its former congregation sold the Sheridan Theater in the early 1970s, it was converted into a Spanish-language theater called the Teatro El Palacio. This operated until the 1990s, after which it closed. While many plans were put forward to repurpose the old theater, it was ultimately demolished, with a senior citizen home standing on the site today.

Still a part of Uptown into the 1980s, Edgewater experienced its own crippling wave of Urban Renewal. Pictured here is a multistory apartment building in the middle of demolition while a distressed onlooker holds up a building permit. Rather than rehab aging apartment buildings, developers during this time opted instead to simply demolish them.

Fires, neglect, and outright abandonment led to some horrific scenes in post–World War II Uptown. Pictured here in the summer of 1967 are three children playing amongst the wreckage of a ruined apartment building. Trash was scattered amongst the bricks and twisted metal, making it no place for children.

A group of four unidentified children pose for a photographer in 1967. Their disheveled and dirty appearance was not uncommon for Uptown by this time as poverty choked the neighborhood. Small bits of debris littered the ground around them.

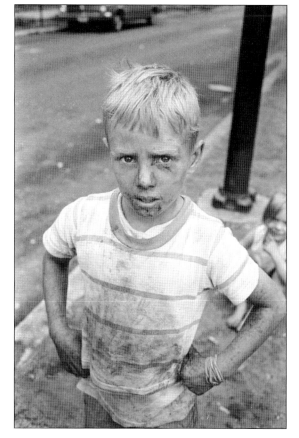

A young boy stands defiantly with his hands on his hips. Behind the dirt and grime on his face, his eyes gaze up at the camera with a sad sort of resilience. His younger sister peeks up at the photographer from the lower-right-hand side.

The 1960s and 1970s saw a massive shift in Uptown's demographics. As tens of thousands of Native American and Appalachian migrants poured into the neighborhood, the face of Uptown began to shift dramatically. Pictured here in the 1970s, a group of American Indians march down Broadway on Thanksgiving, the Buena Memorial Presbyterian Church looming large behind them.

Proudly displaying symbols of their heritage such as drums and traditional fringe clothing, Uptown's newest residents bring awareness to the plight of their community. A large American flag is also brandished, loudly reinforcing their status as proud US citizens.

Community leader Mitchell Whiterabbit was photographed in front of the American Indian Center in 1974. Located at 1630 Wilson Avenue, the center was squarely situated in a highly residential area, offering the Native American community a respite from the hostility they faced in their new surroundings.

A member of the Winnebago Tribe, Whiterabbit was born near Black River Falls in Minnesota. He eventually became a prominent minister before establishing the American Indian Center of St. Paul. He would travel across the Midwest, making stops at other such centers, including, of course, Uptown Chicago's.

Native American children pose with Mitchell Whiterabbit at the American Indian Center's Head Start program. These centers provided essential services for its community, offering day care and further education in addition to afterschool programs. Uptown would soon see a surplus of such social services as it became a port for recently arrived immigrants and migrants.

Here, Whiterabbit poses with two children outside the American Indian Center. Sporting traditional dress, these children would have been encouraged to embrace their culture and celebrate their heritage in their new neighborhood, a far cry from the unspeakable horrors seen in the reeducation schools of previous decades.

The 1960s saw many famous Uptown buildings repurposed. Shown here in the autumn of 1969, the Aragon Ballroom hosts a massive flea market displaying every kind of ware imaginable.

Bustling with locals, the market offered everything from antiques to buttons, silver serving sets to portrait photography. Perhaps more importantly, markets such as these provided a strong sense of community, bringing all manner of Uptown residents together.

The political unrest of the decade brought organized protests to Uptown. A group of residents protest outside the Urban Progress Center, decrying the lack of housing and jobs available in the neighborhood. Ironically, the center was located in the Montrose Beach Hotel on Montrose Avenue, which was eventually demolished for a high rise.

The 1960s also brought the decay of infrastructure. Here, a crumbling viaduct along a major east-west artery is prepared for demolition and replacement. This sort of neglect was a common site for Uptown in the postwar years.

Even into the 1970s, the Clarendon Beach pavilion remained a popular hangout for teens. No longer the most popular beach in the city, its expansive shore maimed by Lake Shore Drive, Clarendon Beach became a place where Uptown teenagers could stay out of trouble. While the pavilion remained intact for a time, its imposing towers and Doric colonnade were removed not long after this photograph was taken, leaving the once grand beach facility little more than a plain brick box.

The recently completed Weiss Memorial Hospital. Opened in 1953 atop what used to be Clarendon Beach, the Mid-century-style hospital offered 236 beds to the Uptown community. Until the early 2000s, Weiss was part of the greater University of Chicago hospital systems, after which it was eventually sold to a California-based, for-profit health provider.

Seen here is another example of a dickie front, this time on or near Argyle Street. Pictured in the 1970s, the combination of classical Western architecture with Asian typeface and businesses showcases the demographic shift Uptown was experiencing at this time.

Broadway near Argyle Street in the 1980s. The New Asian Bank demonstrates the network of businesses opened by and for the recent influx of refugees from Vietnam and Cambodia. To the left of the bank, a parking lot has been carved out.

Having been originally settled as a tiny village known as Argyle, many of the buildings constructed in this part of Uptown reflected the British origins of its residents. Here, a commercial building at Broadway and Argyle features a crenelated battlement tower. A large Modernist office building looks strikingly out of place in the background, clashing with the historic structures around it.

Residents of Asia on Argyle celebrate Chinese New Year in the 1980s or 1990s. A traditional Chinese lion puppet steals the show as onlookers peek out through their windows at the top of the building in the background. These kinds of festivities became commonplace as recently arrived immigrants fought to retain their culture and traditions.

Further north in what is regarded today as Andersonville, an elderly woman sweeps the sidewalk dressed in Swedish costume. Despite the breaking up of Chicago's tightly knit ethnic neighborhoods, many remained steadfast in preserving their heritage.

Five

UPTOWN TODAY

In the last 10 years or so, interest in Uptown has grown. With its plethora of entertainment venues, unique architecture, rich confluence of cultures, and relatively healthy amount of public transportation, the neighborhood has become increasingly attractive to young Chicagoans. Events such as Uptown Art Week and the summertime Uptown Farmer's Market and Argyle Night Market encourage a sense of community while showcasing some of the best that Uptown has to offer.

Several housing developments, such as an infill of the Weis Memorial Hospital parking lot, are bringing hundreds of new rental units to the area, reversing some of the damage wrought by Urban Renewal. Meanwhile, at the western edge of Uptown, a low-slung commercial strip along Clark Street is slowly being transformed by multistory apartment buildings. Although some of these are more expensive, the sheer bulk of new housing should eventually help to keep rent down, as was the case in the early days of Uptown.

This new growth does come at an unfortunate cost, however; with more and more people moving to Uptown, many of its poorer long-time residents are being pushed out, unable to afford the hike in rent. Several SROs (single occupancy rooms), a vital form of housing for low-income residents, have been gutted and transformed into trendy micro condos. The same fate has befallen the former Sheridan Trust & Savings Bank. For several decades, the upper floors of the defunct bank housed nonprofits geared toward the less fortunate members of Uptown, many of whom were forced to relocate after the building was renovated into luxury apartments.

Despite the lessons learned from Urban Renewal, historic structures including already existing apartment buildings are still being demolished in favor of glass-box high rises, threatening the aesthetic and historic character of Uptown. Several once-bustling intersections are still marred by enormous parking lots as the city desperately clings to its dependence on cars. Traffic clogs the streets of Uptown as rail and bus service is continually cut, even as multiple renovations are being undertaken on the nearby elevated train stations.

While Uptown may be thriving in many ways, it has a long way to go before it catches up to its 1920s zenith.

Looking northeast down Clifton Avenue from Broadway in 2023. Between the Sheridan Trust & Savings Bank and the Uptown Broadway Building, all retail has been demolished. What once was a dense commercial corridor has been reduced to extra parking. The brand-new elevated tracks of the Red Line are visible in the distance, as is a generic mid-century high rise. On the back of the former bank, the symbol of a local developer has been painted, signaling its takeover of the iconic Uptown landmark.

In front of the Riviera Theater, a public art piece by artist Lowell Dennis Thompson was added in the 2010s to commemorate the widening of the sidewalk. In order to make the tricky intersection of Racine Avenue and Broadway safer for pedestrians, the sidewalk was widened into something of a public plaza, while bollards protect those on foot from passing cars. Work also included reducing Racine Avenue to a one-way street. At the top of the Riviera, its once ornate parapet has been removed and replaced with a flat, painted version.

Although plans were announced in the late 2010s to restore the Uptown Theater to its former glory, the COVID-19 pandemic effectively squashed the effort. Its intricate keyhole parapet has long since been removed, as has its multistory marquee. To the left, the Green Mill has been chopped up into multiple retail and restaurant spaces, although it does survive in a much smaller capacity.

Formerly packed full of retail in the 1920s, this lot at Clifton Avenue and Lawrence Avenue was eventually gutted to provide parking for the bank next door. A banner encouraging one to "Explore Uptown" has been affixed to the fencing. Behind the lot, the original Northwestern Elevated tracks are in the process of being demolished, with the new ones going up next to them. Lawrence Station, formerly located to the left of the lot, has also been razed and is expected to be rebuilt by 2025.

Another parking lot, this one located at Lawrence Avenue and Winthrop Avenue across the street from the Aragon Ballroom. Formerly the site of a dense apartment and retail block, the lot is an example of how badly Urban Renewal scarred the landscape of Uptown. The small attendant's booth in the lot's center suggests demolition took place in the 1950s. A sign indicates $30 parking for the Aragon, a sign of how car-dependent Uptown and, by extension, the rest of the city has become.

As automobiles gained popularity after World War II, cities saw fit to demolish dense housing and retail in order to cater to the needs of drivers. Here, at Lawrence and Kenmore Avenues, a multistory, mixed-use development was replaced with a strip mall and parking lot. In the background, the former Insurance Exchange Building looms large, now known as the Institute of Cultural Affairs.

At Sheridan Road and Lawrence Avenue, we see yet another instance of apartments and commercial buildings having been long demolished in favor of a strip mall. The unfinished side of the former Lawrence House Hotel is now exposed, as is the large apartment building on the right-hand side of the image. In place of local shops and eateries, the strip hosts a banking chain, a physical therapy facility, and multiple fast-food restaurants.

Adjacent to the Insurance Exchange Building at Sheridan Road and Lakeside Place sits the defunct Lakeside Theater. Closed in 1967, the theater served as a dance studio for Columbia College Chicago before it was converted into a youth center. This led to its once peaked parapet being flattened, while its attached retail until were covered by mosaic tiles. However, this image shows construction work beginning to turn the space into a theater once again.

An example of a recent demolition, this building at Sheridan Road and Leland Avenue demonstrates that historic structures are still being torn down or altered in Uptown to this day. Showcasing a practice known as Facadism, the building's original "skin" was retained, while apartment units were stacked on top. The ground floor showcases the building's red brick and even retains some of its original terra-cotta decoration, seen here at the corners of its parapet and sculpted mask. The Sheridan Plaza stands on the lefthand side of the image. To the left of the former hotel sits the Hotel Grasmere; built in 1915 and designed by architect R.C. Harris, the Grasmere was one of Uptown's first apartment hotels.

A new, larger apartment building has replaced the Classical Revival iteration from the 1910s. After the original building was demolished in the 1960s, a single-story commercial unit took its place, which itself was demolished in the early 2020s to make way for this new one. While not as ornate as its predecessor, Platform 4611 was developed as a transit-oriented apartment building thanks to its proximity to the Wilson elevated station, as well as the 81 and 36 bus lines that run down Wilson Avenue and Broadway respectively.

Finally, at the southeast corner of Wilson Avenue and Broadway, the small United department store was demolished sometime after the 1960s. As a further testament to the ways in which Urban Renewal and car dependency ripped apart Uptown, a dense building at the one of the city's busiest intersections was demolished for a parking-oriented strip mall. Thankfully, with Uptown in the midst of a development boom, there have been suggestions to redevelop this crucial intersection into a mixed-use apartment building.

DISCOVER THOUSANDS OF LOCAL HISTORY BOOKS FEATURING MILLIONS OF VINTAGE IMAGES

Arcadia Publishing, the leading local history publisher in the United States, is committed to making history accessible and meaningful through publishing books that celebrate and preserve the heritage of America's people and places.

Find more books like this at
www.arcadiapublishing.com

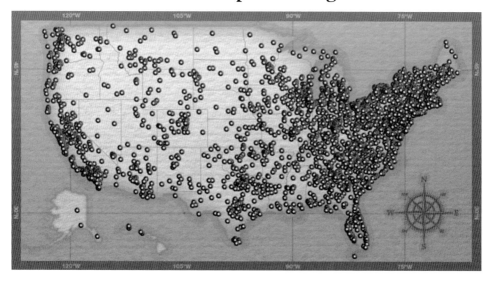

Search for your hometown history, your old stomping grounds, and even your favorite sports team.